Adapted from RANGO: The Movie Story Book
by Justine and Ron Fontes

Based on the Screenplay written by John Logan

Story by
John Logan, Gore Verbinski and James Ward Byrkit

Meet ... the animals from RANGO

The town of **Dirt** is in the **Mojave Desert**. The animals in Dirt don't have very much water.

Roadkill is an armadillo. He lives in the desert.

ROADKILL

The Mayor is a tortoise. The animals of Dirt go to the Mayor for help. But is he good or bad?

THE MAYOR

BAD BILL

Bad Bill is a lizard. He works for the Mayor. He does not like new animals in his town.

BEANS

Beans is a lizard. She has some land but no water. But why does the Mayor want to buy her land?

Everyone is frightened of **Rattlesnake Jake**.

RATTLESNAKE JAKE

RANGO

Rango is a green chameleon. But why is he here? And is he a hero?

SHERIFF

Before you read …
What do you think? Who is going to be the new Sheriff of Dirt?

New Words

What do these new words mean? Ask your teacher or use your dictionary.

city

Look at the **city**!

bar

The man walked into the **bar**.

hero

He is a **hero**.

bird

Look at the **bird**!

kill

Cats **kill** small animals.

land

He has a lot of **land**.

mud

I love **mud**!

pipe

The **pipe** is for water.

story

Listen to the **story**!

water tower

This is a **water tower**.

'hiss'

Hiss!

Verbs

Present	Past
fall	fell
find	found
think	thought

CHAPTER ONE
The chameleon

It was very hot in the Mojave Desert. A chameleon walked in the hot sun. Who was he? Where was he from?

'Hello, friend!' someone said. It was Roadkill, the armadillo.

'Where can I find water?' asked the chameleon.

'In the town,' Roadkill said. 'It's one day's walk from here.'

Next day, the chameleon came to the town of Dirt. He was hot, tired and thirsty.

He walked into a bar. There were a lot of animals there. They stopped talking and looked at him.

'Give me some water!' the chameleon said.

Everyone laughed.

'There's no water in this town,' someone said. 'Who are you?'

The chameleon started thinking … quickly.

'I'm … Rango,' he said.

'Did you kill the Jenkins brothers?' someone asked.

'Yes, that was me!' said Rango.

'Did you kill all seven brothers?'

'Of course!' he said. And he started the story. Rango loved a good story. And the animals in the bar loved a hero.

But not everyone liked Rango's story.

'You killed the Jenkins brothers,' Bad Bill said, 'But what about me?'

Rango and Bad Bill walked out of the bar into the sun.

'What am I going to do?' thought Rango.

Suddenly, Rango saw a very big bird. Bad Bill ran. Rango ran too, but the bird went after him.

'Help!' shouted Rango, and ran into the old water tower. The water tower fell onto the bird.

The animals were very happy. Now Rango was a hero!

CHAPTER TWO
The Mayor

The Mayor was with a girl lizard. Her name was Beans.

'Listen, Beans,' said the Mayor. 'Your land is not good. You don't have any water. I can buy your land from you.'

'No!' said Beans.

Then the Mayor saw Rango. He wanted to talk to him.

'Ah, Mr Rango,' he said. 'When you have water, you have everything.'

The Mayor had some water on his table, but he did not give any water to Rango.

'You are a hero,' the Mayor said. 'Please be Sheriff of our town!'

The new Sheriff of Dirt! Rango was very happy.

The animals of Dirt waited at the water pipe. They waited for water. But out of the pipe came ... mud.

'What are we going to do?' shouted the animals.

'We're going to look for water,' said Rango. 'Who's coming?'

'Me,' said Beans. 'Where are we going?'

Rango did not know.

'Let's find the end of the water pipe,' said an old bird.

'Yes!' shouted Rango. 'We're going to the end of the water pipe!'

The Mayor watched. 'It's time for Rattlesnake Jake!' he said to Bad Bill.

Rango and the animals went to the end of the pipe. They found some mud.

'I don't understand it!' said Rango. 'We don't have water … but we have mud.'

'Everyone's thirsty,' said Beans, 'but the Mayor has water. I don't understand that!'

'I'm going to talk to the Mayor,' Rango said.

CHAPTER THREE
Rattlesnake Jake

Rango and the animals came back to town. Suddenly everyone ran away.

'HISSSSSSSSSSSS!'

Rango saw a very big snake with red eyes. It was Rattlesnake Jake.

Rango was very frightened.

'You're not a hero, Sheriff,' said Rattlesnake Jake. 'Did you kill the Jenkins brothers … all seven of them?'

'No, I didn't,' said Rango quietly.

'Go away from this town,' shouted Rattlesnake Jake, 'and never come back!'

Rango had no answer this time. He walked away slowly.

Rattlesnake Jake laughed. He went to see the Mayor.

The Mayor had some pictures of a new city in front of him. Beans was there too.

'You can't have my land!' Beans shouted.

Rattlesnake Jake hissed, 'Give your land to the Mayor.'

Rango was sad. He walked and walked.

'Hello, friend!' someone said. It was Roadkill. 'Come and see this.'

Rango looked. It was the big city of Las Vegas. There was a lot of water in Las Vegas.

Rango thought about the Mayor … and Beans' land …

Suddenly Rango started to look for something. Soon he found it – a big water pipe.

'Look!' he shouted. 'Someone closed the pipe. Now I understand! The Mayor wants to have a new city on the land. He doesn't want the town of Dirt.'

CHAPTER FOUR
The hero

Beans looked into Rattlesnake Jake's red eyes. She was very frightened. Suddenly, there was a shout.

'Rattlesnake Jake, come out here!'
It was Rango.
'This is going to be interesting!' said Jake.
He went out. Beans and the Mayor went with him. Rango was next to the water pipe.

'Are you thirsty?' asked Rango.

Back in the desert, Roadkill shouted, 'Now!'

Suddenly, a lot of water came out of the pipe and fell on Jake.

The Mayor looked at the water and started thinking ... quickly.

'Rango,' he said. 'You and me ... Let's be friends! And Rattlesnake Jake? He's nothing.'

But Jake was behind the Mayor.

'Good work, Rango,' Jake said. Then he looked at the Mayor. 'And you are coming with me. HISSSSSSSSSSSSSSSSSSSS!'

And no one in the town saw the Mayor again.

The animals were happy. They jumped up and down in the beautiful water.

Beans looked into Rango's eyes.

'Thank you,' she said. 'You are our hero!'

THE END

Real World

THE MOJAVE DESERT

The Mojave Desert is in California, in the south west of the United States.

The **Sierra Nevada mountains** are on the west of the desert. The rain from the sea does not come to the desert because of the mountains. The desert has only a few centimetres of rain every year.

People

In the 1900s, men and women came to California from the east. They wanted to find work and land. Some of them found land in the Mojave Desert. But there was not very much water and life was very hard for them.

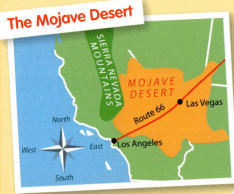

The Mojave Desert

Did you know?

It is very hot in the Mojave Desert. In July and August, it is sometimes 50°C in the day and 38°C at night.

Animals

The **Mojave Rattlesnake** lives in the mountains. It is about one metre long.

The **Desert Tortoise** usually lives for eighty to one hundred years. In July and August it stays underground.

There are lots of **lizards** in the desert. Lizards can live for a long time with no water.

Would you like to go to the desert? Why / Why not?

What do these words mean? Find out.
mountains   underground
people   life   hard

After you read

1 **Match the names with the animals.**

   a) Rango
   b) The Mayor
   c) Beans
   d) Roadkill
   e) Jake

   i) armadillo
   ii) lizard
   iii) rattlesnake
   iv) tortoise
   v) chameleon

2 **Are these facts about Rango true (✓) or false (✗)? Write in the box.**

   a) He comes from Dirt. ✗
   b) He walked into a bar. ☐
   c) He killed the Jenkins brothers. ☐
   d) He killed the big bird. ☐
   e) He saw Las Vegas. ☐
   f) He found the water. ☐
   g) He killed Rattlesnake Jake. ☐
   h) He is a hero! ☐

   Where's the popcorn?
   Look in your book.
   Can you find it?

Puzzle time!

1 Read and write the words. The first letter of each word is in a star.

a) There is no water here.   d e s e r t
b) This animal can fly.   _ _ _ _
c) Water comes to your house in this.   _ _ _ _
d) There are a lot of houses here.   _ _ _ _
e) You find this in the park after rain.   _ _ _

2 In the story, who is good and who is bad? Give the characters a score out of five.
(5 = very good, 1 = very bad)

Beans

Rango

The Mayor

Bad Bill

Rattlesnake Jake

3 Complete the speech bubbles.

a: When you have water, you have ....

b: We don't have water but we ....

c: This is going to be .... !

d: You can't have .... !

4 Draw your favourite character. Then complete the sentences about the character.

For example: Rango has ......**big eyes**...... .

a) He / She is ....

b) He / She has ....

c) He / She likes ....

Imagine...

1 Work in groups. Choose a character.

2 Your teacher is going to read Chapter Three and Chapter Four of *Rango*. Listen and mime your character.

Chant

1 **Listen and read.**

Rattlesnake Jake

Rattlesnake Jake
Has small, red eyes.
Rattlesnake Jake
Has a big black hat.
Rattlesnake Jake
Has a terrible laugh.
Rattlesnake Jake
Is bad, bad, bad!

2 **Say the chant.**